Secret Places of Trout Fishermen

GEORGE MENDOZA

Secret Places of

Trout Fishermen

Macmillan Publishing Co., Inc.
NEW YORK

Collier Macmillan Publishers
LONDON

"Against the Current in Chile" first appeared in *Fly Fisherman Magazine* in June 1975.
"Fishing with Hemingway in Spain" first appeared in *Fly Fisherman Magazine* in April 1977.
"Fly Fishing for Trophy Tuna" first appeared in *Sports Afield* in July 1977.
"For Charles Ritz, from Yugoslavia" first appeared in *Gray's Sporting Journal* in winter 1977.
"Test and Itchen Diary" first appeared in *Gray's Sporting Journal* in winter 1976.

Photo credits: Paul Heverin, Courtesy of Irish Tourist Board, p. 6, p. 27, pp. 76–79; Adrian Dufflocq, p. 7, p. 8; Dermot Wilson, pp. 20–24, 70–71; American Sportsman (copyright © 1977. All rights reserved American Broadcasting Companies, Inc.), p. 90.

Unless otherwise indicated, all photographs are by NICOLE SEKORA-MENDOZA.

Macmillan Publishing Co., Inc.
866 Third Avenue, New York, N.Y. 10022
Collier Macmillan Canada, Ltd.

Library of Congress Cataloging in Publication Data

Mendoza, George.
    Secret places of trout fishermen.

    1. Mendoza, George—Biography. 2. Authors, American
—20th century—Biography. 3. Trout fishing. I. Title.
PS3563.E49Z524   811'.5'4 [B]   77-22442
ISBN 0-02-584300-1

FIRST PRINTING 1977

Printed in the United States of America

for RAY ROBERTS

after four years and a lifetime

guddling for myself . . .

Contents

Contents

THERE'S NO ENDING

Preface

IT seems as though I have spent my whole life working and playing at my book, *Secret Places of Trout Fishermen*. Now the work is done. The poems I've felt, the rivers I've touched, the long flights across the world to reach a lonely river—the surge of my heart when a stream was near, all these gather together like the memory of a song.

I am a romantic and a poet, a man unafraid to be inside himself, where the journey is under the dark and against the sea. I am propelled by the unkown, for to follow the path cleared is the mountain removed, the mysteries of the stars gone, a flower no longer wild in the grasses hiding.

Somtimes I despair that I have not given more days to an old farmhouse by a stream where woods, deep and secret, walk through you. For this was my soul's way beyond the cages of the city.

I confess I have lived my life for myself and my book is like my farmhouse down a poppy road of dreams where poplars and maples golden stir the wind.

I do not ask you to go my way. Yet I know the heart of a child will some day find me, and a lover in spring-bloom will know me from my poems-ago, though I not be there—

GEORGE MENDOZA
Paris—November 1976

Acknowledgments

I am deeply grateful to all the fishing souls who helped in the gentle casts of my book: Ed Zern, *Field and Stream*; Don Zahner, *Fly Fisherman*; David Maxey, *Sports Afield*; Ed Gray, *Gray's Sporting Journal*; Robert Shnayerson, *Quest*; Roone Arledge, *The American Sportsman*; Richard Kagan, *Town and Country*; Nelson Bryant, *New York Times*; Dermot Wilson, Charles Ritz, Adrian Dufflocq, Slim Pickens, John S. Hilson, Douglas Reid, John Groth, Odd Haraldsen, Dudley Soper, and especially my friend Bud Frasca of *Freshet Press*.

I would also like to express my thanks to the many airlines who got me to the streams around the world: TWA, Air France, SAS, Braniff International, Pan American, Air Canada, Lufthansa, Iberia, Aer Lingus, and British Airways.

Long Ago a Boy

A lone bird in the mist, British Columbia.

The Fish That Got Away

*W*HEN I was about nine years old my father rented a summer cottage by a brook in Jamaica, Vermont. The brook was wide and shallow, and downstream there was an iron bridge crossing where the water suddenly became mysterious and deep.

The brook was like a wild child tumbling spring-cold from the Green Mountains, its banks filtered with fern and birch and alder leaves. I remember the finger-deep coves near the edge of the bank that sheltered minnows and little trout. Here, as a boy from the city, I came to dream, to drift, to get lost in a world I had never known before.

I did not know it then but that brook was to shape my life forever. It was to make poetry of my manhood, turn all my being onto the course of natural things—stars in the eyes of fish, pebbles in the grass and the sound of wind in dreams. It made me a romantic, a lover, a gypsy.

All that summer it seemed I spent my time wandering from one rock to the next along that brook. Upstream I went and downstream, discovering, listening, sometimes falling asleep with the song of the brook playing in my head.

A trout would splash and I would feel a wild sensation come over me. What was the fish seeking? The mystery of this underwater creature suddenly blooming in air like a bird, then gone into the pebbly depths. *How can I catch you?* I wondered, *bring you to my hands?*

My first trout rod was a wobbly metal contraption with a reel wound with black string that looked more like a toy for Central Park goldfishing. But I took that rod and reel seriously; indeed I did, as I had assured myself that this was the rod and reel that would take my first trout.

I went back to the place where I had seen that glorious trout appear, and, sticking a sweet worm on my hook, I cast for the fish. It was a sloppy cast and my worm went everywhere but into the water. Again a worm, again a cast.

Nothing happened. Where was that fish hiding? I tried again and again, hoping my fish would reward me for my efforts. I had about given up hope, thinking that this brook held no fish, at least no fish for me, when suddenly a tug, a great shock came into my hand—a fish! I had hooked into my fish!

That trout leaped and thrashed, how he leaped and thrashed, a brook trout of about twelve gleaming inches, a garden of flowers growing out of his silvery sides. I couldn't believe my eyes. Then I felt my knees and legs begin to tremble, my hand and arm quivered down into my heart and it seemed as though I could hear the trout talk to me: *You'll not hold me, wandering boy, but this day I'll give you a memory that will haunt you for all your days.*

I've got you now, I had thought. He had flopped upon a nest of rocks in a shallow of the brook. I remember I had just begun to reach for him when he wiggled free of the hook. For a stunned moment I could only watch him slip slowly back into the water.

Frantically I fell upon the fish with my whole body. I wanted that trout. More than anything in the world I wanted that trout to be mine forever.

I don't know how my fish got away but he did, and I've been looking for him in brooks and rivers and ponds and along banks ever since that time.

I know he's somewhere, big and strong and beautiful. I tell myself he will never be caught. And if he has been hooked, he got away as he did when he was young and a daring fighter.

Something else too, a secret thought:

I don't think I'll ever find my trout, and in my heart I hope I never will. If I did, maybe the haunting road of river calling would be gone, and a brook would come to be only the bones of a long-ago time. I would never want that to happen, so I keep searching.

> I hear splashing
> under a tree.
> Trout rolls over
> like a crescent moon
> in the water dark.
> If you see my eyes

Long Ago a Boy

> by a river bank
> I have come a-searching
> like a gypsy boy.

Sailor Searching for a Brook

*A*FTER that summer I never wanted to leave Vermont. I begged my father to buy a farm-house, to give up the city and dig into the wild country. I'd do anything to live where there were meadows and flowers and streams to follow, and my fish still to catch.

We even looked at a few houses as I remember, but my father explained how unrealistic I was being.

"We're not of the Vermont marrow," my father had said. "You're the son of a Spaniard born and we'd be foreigners here until the prophets wrote the next Bible."

I didn't understand my father's words. What did my being Spanish and Irish have to do with living among the gentle folk of Vermont?

"You'll learn the American way when you return to this coun-

try someday," my father had warned me and that was the end
of Vermont for many long summers.

> You were born in Chicago,
> were you stranger?
> You were born in Ohio,
> were you stranger?
> You were born in Texas,
> were you stranger?
> If you didn't know where you were born,
> you wouldn't be a stranger.
> You'd be a flute player
> looking for the back of a tree.
> You'd be a poet spinner
> flying with a yellow finch.
> You'd be a lean and handsome lover
> loving every loving thing.

A few years later we moved from New York and settled in
Stony Brook, Long Island, a reconstructed Revolutionary village
surrounded by seawater tides, endless grass flats, screaming gulls,
and intoxicating smells from the ocean.

Schooners and square riggers had put into this port around
the turn of the century; this romantic reality made the little village authentic and not really anything else.

Here I learned the ways of the sea and I became a sailor and
a swimmer and built my own sailboat.

Out on my boat wearing my black turtleneck, I felt like Jack
London; I had the look of an adventurer and thought that as
long as the world was wild and full of nature then I would
be free.

When I went sailing I always took along my rusty old Ver-

When I was fourteen I wanted to sail around the world.
A few years later, I found myself lost at sea in my
thirteen-foot Old Town sloop.

mont trout rod, for I loved to troll for mackerel and weakfish while my little sloop ran before a good breeze. Summer days and nights on into the fall I was a boy sail bent and fishing out the ocean. I believe I must have caught and eaten every kind of fish, clam, crab, or eel there was, but something was missing in this basketful of happiness.

I was still yearning for my trout and for my brook. I was a sailor on an ocean as deep as God's voice, but all the while I was looking for a mountain slide of stream, a run of freshwater rocks, the spongy bank full of shadow drift and whispers.

I was seeking the magical, wandering trout born out of a poet's noonday dream, fiercely colored by a meadow painter and let to fly in the sky called stream, called brook, called river, where men become boys again.

Parachute Man

I SEE a man grown up now, perhaps standing in his boyhood footprints, standing beside a dam under a moon-filled Battenkill night. In the tops of the trees the September wind stirs the leaves and the man is filled with the turning leaves. He feels the wind cool against his face. It's a good time for thinking and being still and alone.

In the soft darkness the man reflects on the life behind him: adventures and agonies, pleasures and the prices he paid for them, all gone as though taken by the currents of a stream. Everything seems so far away now, the city, work, family—and time.

Here it all dissolves. Alone, a man alone with a river he loves, a river he keeps coming back to in search of brown trout among the night stone.

Before I entered the river I gave my Payne a gentle twitch—a sweet and powerful rod, a treasure of wood few men possess. I had tied on a White Miller, a favorite of mine for this late hour of night, a fly that would inject frenzy into a trout foraging for moths and frogs.

Soundlessly, I made my way to the spillway of the dam and, breathing deeply all the smells of the night, I cast my line to the river. I could see the fly cock up in the moonlight, a White Miller feathery in the surface film, and I let it float a while. Then, quietly picking up the line, I cast again, this time a little bit farther.

The moonlight was brilliant, and I knew the trout would not be fooled easily tonight. I felt like an Indian stalking my fish. As the night grew on I had a strange and sudden feeling that someone was watching me.

I kept looking about, imagining unfamiliar sounds. But I wanted more time there, in the solitary quiet. So I stayed, though prickly fears made me keep looking behind and above.

Suddenly my line came to life with tremendous force. Then the fish rose out of the water; a monster. I had gotten into a spectacular fish.

That fish ran and jumped till it seemed he could run and jump no more. I'd reel him up and out he would streak again. I had never known a fish like this in all my life. Finally, I could feel he was beginning to tire; his runs and frantic leaps were now flickering lights of a fierce fighter.

I kept telling myself it would be over soon. I was going to win. I couldn't make myself believe I was actually going to get that fish in.

I double-checked everything mentally: my leader was fresh,

Wading into the shadows of my thoughts,
Boulder River, Montana.

I had cut back to four-pound strength for the night, my fly had been tied on so that it would never let go unless the good Lord himself had decided to return as fish and battle it out with man. Now it was all that I had learned or what I hadn't learned against all the fighting will of that fish to remain alive.

The time had come, the fish was tired, so I reached behind me for my net and with one great scooping motion I had my trout.

I was shaking with joy. The trout had to be at least five pounds, maybe more. I couldn't wait to take it to the inn and show my wife. Carefully, but firmly, I gripped the great trout so that I could remove the fly from its lip. And just at the moment when the fish was unhooked there was a voice behind me.

"That's a beautiful trout!"

I was so startled, terrified to hear a human voice, that I dropped the trout into the river.

"Oh God!" I shouted into the night. "I lost my fish!"

"My gosh," said the strange voice. "I didn't mean to scare you."

"Well—you did," I stammered, "and you made me . . ." I was so filled with anguish I couldn't express what I was feeling.

The stranger was a huge and powerful man, a fisherman. A man who loved to fish for brown trout among the night stone.

"I don't know what to say," said the man. "But you really weren't going to keep that beautiful trout anyway, were you?"

"You're damn right I was going to keep it," I muttered, still angry.

"You know," said the man, "it's bad luck to keep a great fish like that, to keep a trout of such beauty. You might not take another for many days to come."

I turned from the intruder. "After losing that fish I don't

think I want to try anymore."

"That's nonsense! Now here, you take some of my flies and try them tomorrow morning. You'll see what I'm talking about!"

In the man's open hand I beheld some of the most beautiful flies I had ever seen.

"What are they called?" I asked.

"Parachutes," he said. "They fall upon the water like milkweed. You take them; go on, try them on the Atherton stretch tomorrow and let me know how you do."

I never asked for the parachute man's name, nor did he ask for mine, and that made me think about the trout that had gotten away. I was glad he was free, although his freedom was only an accident. But then so was his capture, for I'm not that good a fisherman.

"As Though I Were a Thief with Time"

I come to this mystical brook-river
to escape awhile,
to take my drink as though I were a thief with time:
to dream by the brook-drifting bank,
to cloud my head in clouds,
sailing on the dark brook-rippled top,
to tie a speck of winged fly
to a leader silken as a fair girl's hair,
to walk across fresh-cut fields of rye and wheat
to a stretch the poet Soper said was fast, so deep
and sun-gold, like the tassled corn,
to talk to a friend, my poet friend,
under a brook-moon with stars dusting themselves
like crystal dew spanning the yards of the Dipper.

Fishermen crave for their names to mark a pool, a run somewhere.
Atherton has his stretch on a turn of the Battenkill and I remember
taking a beauty there. My name is in the wind through the canyons of
the Boulder and the pools are many and deep and all nameless.

Long Ago a Boy

O let the world spin old.
My dawn is sweet,
September-cold.
Mist-wind is creeping low
as a serpent with its head under a rock
and its tail still weaving in the grass.
On the brook before the flower's opened
I'm casting by the dam,
old dam, weather-planked by the burned-down mill
where yellow butterflies flutter above charred timbers
and by the stream wild trout lilies and boneset and mint
tilt like windmills,
and clover balls pop like little plums in the brush weed.

The smell of the brook is swimming in my head,
my soul reaches for a somewhere prayer.
I know the lunkers are nymphing from the deeps,
but before the morning wind is up
I'll be wandering like a gypsy boy down the stretch below,
where the white house high on the birch bank
peeps through the peeling trees,
where the brook-river bends like a bough
and the alder leaves drop in the brook-furrows
to ride and play beside my fly.

Fishing the Morning Lonely

*W*HEN I wade into a river fishing for trouts I feel as though I am entering another part of my soul. And as I watch the early lights flower in the shadows, I know I have come to the river seeking more, much more than the catching of the trouts.

How can I describe this to you—you who have fished the morning lonely and you who were never there?

I must relate an experience I had while picking my way among the stones downstream. The morning was glorious, coming up creamy colored mayflies.

It was a day to follow a brook, to drift every thought in your head out into the currents, to walk with the water, to glide upon it like a cloud.

Reflections of trees and flowers floated on the surface of the brook in a million images of flashing loveliness. *Truly*, I thought, *here is the face of God, in all this and not beyond this.*

Under the trees on the opposite bank it was dark, full of lost whispers, and there were trouts coming up, ripples of big and little trouts in pools scattered like wild flowers, unaware of a stalk of man sticking out of the river.

I was very quiet. I said to the river:

I have no name, no place have I come from and nowhere do I go yet I am with you like one of your own rocks and I have come to take one of your fish.

Water swirled round the pilings of my boots, pressing hard against my legs. I felt like a boy again, adventuring along my first Vermont brook. It was the kind of day that I hoped would last forever, a day of wine and fruit and song.

Across the river I saw a huge dorsal fin slash the surface of a pool, and I could feel my chest suddenly expand with excitement.

I wanted to play that fish. A careful cast placed above him and the bamboo would soon be bending and my reel singing out.

I tied on a sulphur parachute, waxed it lightly with my fingers, then let it drop on the water so that I could evaluate its float. The wings of the parachute shot straight up, a natural fly, none better to take the trout.

I started to cast upstream, quartering my line across and up, mending the line quickly left to avoid the deadly, sudden drag.

It was all working, rod and line a ballet, every cast coming closer to the trout. Now I could see the fly sailing over his pool, and I could feel that fish as though my heart were at the end of the line. I told myself he was ready to leap for my delicate fly.

Boulder River, Montana—she doesn't let go of
your heart.

But he didn't leap for anything. That fly was perfect, I re-assured myself and, picking up my line, I cast above him again. This time I would give the fly a tiny jiggle, make it look alive.

Suddenly a wave of laughter filled the air. And the fish struck at the precise moment of my distraction! He was there and I wasn't and now he had my beautiful parachute and a memory of fine tippet flowing from his lip.

I cursed and on top of that I cursed again. I knew my fish was down and gone. I could almost see him brooding beneath a ledge of darkened stone. He would not come up for a long time.

The laughter rose again stronger round the bend of the pool, and I made my way toward the sounds that had ruined my morning catch.

When we looked at each other across the river none of us could believe the truth absurd. Hadn't we traveled far and long enough to avoid human company?

But there we were, a fisherman fishing the morning lonely, and a boy and girl in the nest of a rubber raft spinning waves of love in the hiding place of a dark brook cove.

What could we say and if we knew what to say—how then to say it?

I looked up into the sky, full of the memory of those lovely open legs.

Adventures—and There Were Some

So we search for trout in many ways and many places, each of us, I suspect, with some secret inward vision, subconscious as often as not, of what trout fishing really is. We will settle for less, often much less, and we may even find other, unexpected experiences more brilliant than the one we seek. I have many friends who never stop traveling in search of trout.

RODERICK HAIG-BROWN

Up in the high, sweet country, Montana! Is
there a fisherman who can ever forget?

Ah, Spring! You've Got Me by the Hand

SPRING is the time for lovers and flowers and trout fishermen. Since I am all three, I must prepare early, for the sounds of the river are near and the trout are waiting.

Winter ices in most fishermen, a time turned to memories of seasons past, a time for tying up rare feathers of birds and the fur of animals to make flies, trout flies and salmon flies, a time for reading more books about the fishing life, a waiting time for spring to come again.

Ah, spring! You've got me by the hand. My canvas trout creel that has waded rivers around the world is out once more. I can see that it's beginning to have a classic, worn look like a vintage car or a fine old wine. I like things that grow old, that touch places and time, marked by memories.

My trout rods are bamboo, not the new graphite that is becoming more fashionable. I take the gleaming sticks out of their leather cases as though I were opening the graves of their master-makers: Garrison, Payne, and Leonard. All gone now. But not the life they left in the wood.

I know it's still too early; the season has not opened yet. There are no rivers below my terrace where a line may float the current. I must appear a fool to my neighbors across the way. *What is that man doing casting line from a piece of wood?*

Ah, spring! You are the wood and I your line. How good it feels to flick the bamboo again even though it be from my terrace overlooking leafless, dusty gardens. Now as I test the wood with my hand cocked firm, I am dreaming I am on my Battenkill in Vermont, casting to the tongues of water below the dam. Trout are rising in the chilling air. I am working a Quill Gordon (Iron Fraudator)* in the heavy currents, and a trout suddenly strikes, a fighter of two pounds, slashing out leader and line, my first trout of the new year.

How soon will it come—opening day? I know of fishermen who drive hundreds of miles to be with their rivers on opening day. It is usually raining and the wind is cold and the water freezing. Many know they will not catch a fish, not one trout will come to their fly. It doesn't matter, nothing matters on opening day except being there by your river. It is a madness that has saved many stark souls.

Meanwhile, there are days and nights still to go: reels must be oiled and played with, lines are greased and new leaders are

* According to Art Flick, my friend and trout-fisherman extraordinaire, the Quill Gordon is the "first mayfly of consequence to emerge, coming rather early in the season, often appearing when the air is so cold that few of the flies are able to leave the water, being numbed and unable to fly."

My old fishing creel, soaking up
the Irish spray.

knotted and fly boxes come open for the feathers will soon be in flight.

As for me, one fisher of the trouts, I am a dreamer from the terrace. If you see my line whipping past your window, I have not come to hook your flowerpots, only time and more dreams.

Against the Current
in Chile

YOU may escape to St. Paul de Vence or Hampshire or a small seacoast village in the north of Spain to muffle the dull drums of the world. But when you tell someone that you've just returned from trout fishing in Chile, watch the incredulous envy swell in their eyes, observe their primordial sense of adventure return, and then be prepared to spin stories about giant trouts rolling for dry flies on rivers called Cumilahue, Calcurrupe, and Nilahue.

And suddenly you'll discover you're walking at the feet of the dreamlike, smoke-drifting Andes where fields of blackberry bushes surround you, dripping with jewel-like rain-washed fruit, and beneath them are flowers mixed with the colors of an Inca rainbow.

For you are now in the backwash of time, almost seven thousand miles from New York City. There are no telephones; a letter may reach you several months late. The nearest village, Llifén, split by a dirt road, seems only to exist in the mind's eye.

But after a few days of wading deep and fast rivers, casting to whale-sized brown trout and rainbows under the Southern Cross, drenching your tongue and spirits with cool Chilean wines, you become aware that it doesn't matter if anything else exists. Somehow you're here, ready to give yourself over to the dream of fishing against the current in Chile.

¡Hola Pescadores!

"Fish to the rise!" said Adrian Dufflocq, a lion among fishermen and owner of the charming and rustic Cumilahue Trout Fishing Lodge. It was a wonderful evening to fish for trouts, the *puelche* wind as soft as the darkness, a star-scattered night like the September nights I remembered along my Vermont streams. A red-beaked torrent duck, seeking nymphs, skittered across a *correntada* and disappeared.

Hoagy was downstream fishing with one of his own beautifully tied stone fly nymphs. I kept thinking about how Hoagy had told my wife he was going to get the "big fish"; a determined trout fisherman indeed! And although we were not fishing against each other, were we deep in our hearts angling for that one trout men dream about, go to the ends of their lives to find, come all the way to little Llifén to cast for? The slashing, striking trout, sleek as a missile, secret and rare as the shy, bell-shaped *copihue*.

"Rises beyond that boulder," cried Adrian. "They're waiting for you, George!" I felt the same old nervousness grip me. *God, I thought, what am I going to do if I actually get into a ten- or fifteen-pound monster?* I could barely see the dry fly now as it sailed, swoosh, swoosh, back and forth in the settling darkness. Then, as I let the line shoot from my Garrison, a trout suddenly exploded out of the water in front of me. I saw it rolling over and over; there seemed to be no end to its power and fury.

For a moment I froze with shock. I couldn't believe that the gentle Cumilahue River held such lunkers! I heard Adrian laughing behind me. "They're in here. You believe, George?"

When we returned to the lodge, chunks of reddish logs chopped from the roble trees were burning upright in the sunken fireplace. Adrian opened a bottle of *Vina Tarapaca* and poured the red delight into small peasant glasses. The wine was as smooth as the night river, and as we sipped our wine and talked about the monster trouts that rose, I noticed that Hoagy was holding onto a substantial length of stick.

"What's that for, making a new Garrison?" I teased my friend, who has as keen a love for the bamboo rod as I.

"That's how big my fish was." Hoagy's eyes twinkled with joy.

"You're kidding. You took one?"

"Released him, but measured him first."

Adrian went over to him and held the stick up before the fire. "At least twenty inches. A good fight, Hoagy?"

"Best I've ever experienced so far," Hoagy beamed boyishly. "Guess we came to the right place."

"And maybe we'll never leave!" I laughed, full of the joy of the evening.

Dinner was announced by a sweetly smiling Chilean servant girl. We sat down to a most delicious meal of carbonara soup—a mixture of beans, squash, potatoes, beef, and a juicy chunk of corn on the cob—and all the while more wine flowed. We found

31

Chile—a world of rivers to run through
your dreams . . .

ourselves talking about life and fishing beyond the time when the lodge's generator conked out, a pleasant failure of machinery that we looked forward to every night exactly at midnight. Candles were lighted and flickered between us as we laughed and talked into the sleepy hours of early morning.

Each day began with the cock crowing the dreams out of your head. You'd open your eyes and look out a large window framing evergreens and *colihue* forests that you knew trailed off to a pool or shade-filled run somewhere. In the distance the peaks of the Andes were mist-capped and powdery white with snow fallen during the night. While the cock broke the stillness of the morning you found yourself remembering patches of pleasurable time since you arrived in Chile: the road-dusty trip to Valdivia where we bought hand-woven Araucanian rugs for the price of a fancy lunch in New York City; the old painted boats that pulled up alongside the stone docks in Valdivia, loaded with pears and apples and peaches, a scene reminiscent of Paris; beautiful young boys and girls smiling in the sunlight. And the food, all the good food! You savored empanadas and the fabulous seafood—erizos, cholgas, locos, but especially the pejerreyes, smelts cooked in butter, drunk with wine as golden as the finest Montrachet. And you thought of the mountains flowering green with *quila* and *colihue* and the flowers you picked from the fields to send to your love. And there was the evening you descended a cliff by rope to fish in the milky river Nilahue where you stood in water layered ten to fifteen feet deep with volcanic ash and sand and lava, and then came back up in the dark through a forest cave.

It was, I remember, at the bottom of the Nilahue Valley that I found a *pancora* shell emptied of life, a cinnamon-colored crustacean native to Chile. How gentle and fragile it seemed in death, its pink claws held out as though in warning.

Your thoughts suddenly turned into yourself and you wondered what there is about trout fishing that is so seductive, endlessly mysterious? What is there in every river that keeps calling my name? Calcurrupe, Caunahue, Nilahue, Cumilahue. Had I seen them in a dream, ice-blue, clear, and cold to the bottom of their stones?

Here I am, sleeping beside these rivers in the warmth and comfort of Adrian's beautiful paradise. But how many more rivers will call out to me, how long is the journey of the endless stream?

At breakfast, Adrian asked me to write a poem for him before I left. He said he would frame it, put it alongside his "Hall of Fame" gallery where smiling men like Ernest Schwiebert hung holding onto fat dead trout. I didn't answer Adrian but I knew my poem would be very quiet, perhaps put into the air and let go.

"Where are we fishing today?" I asked.

"The trail of witches," said Adrian. "We call it Calcurrupe."

"Rainbows?" exclaimed Hoagy.

"Browns and rainbows, big fish and a very dangerous river. My boatman, Bernardino, was drowned in this river last spring."

Hoagy and I looked at each other. "Muddlers and eight-foot rods," we agreed.

"And strong legs!" Adrian smiled. "Let's tie up some flies and conserve our energies until evening."

When men decide to go fishing and spend most of the day

preparing for the evening hatch you may look upon the event as though it were a feast with time. You wax the lines, compare rods, make leaders new again, dab flies with mucilin from England, light up your favorite pipe, and drink lots of coffee.

As Adrian had promised, we tied flies and watched like fascinated students as he tied up the most extraordinary flies I have ever seen.

"You're the Picasso of the fly-tying world!" I announced with gusto.

"Watch out, Adrian," Hoagy warned playfully, "he's after all your flies!"

"He knows they will catch fish!" Adrian grinned. "I weave secret Andean magic into my flies so that when the trout looks up he is hypnotized—he is under my spell."

Toward noon the sun beamed down through the *pelu* and *notro* trees and in the field the *ulmo* was exploding with white petals while bees by the millions were squeezing the yellow coves of the *ulmo*, filling their pollen sacs until they were golden and bursting.

For lunch we had a special treat out on the grass veranda. Adrian's secretary and boatman, Liche, had roasted a freshly killed spring lamb—dripping hot chunks spiked on a long stake. My first bite into that meat convinced me. I had never tasted such utterly delicious lamb. Then, opening a bottle of *Vina San Pedro*, Adrian filled our glasses and toasted, "Tight lines this evening, gentlemen!"

After a superb cup of Chilean nescafe, Adrian advised that we take a siesta, reminding us once again that we would need all our strength to battle the Calcurrupe. I went off into the field to sleep among the flowers.

On the Nilahue, a beautiful brown on the
end of my line.

When evening came we were ready and eager for our adventure on the Calcurrupe. Boots, rods, jackets, nets, and Adrian's old creel were thrown into the back of his truck. We drove along a dirt road for several miles until Adrian turned off at a farm. Gates were opened and closed again so that the cows and sheep would not escape, a good rule for every fisherman to follow.

And then all at once we were at the river's edge. It was a powerful river, deep and thrusting with pools of blue and green shimmering incredibly clear. It was as wide as it was powerful. And the mountains, colihue thickets, and stands of cypress on the far bank drove your breath down into your heart. *This was a river*, you said aloud, *a river of rivers*.

"Gear up!" Adrian called out to us. "It will get dark soon and we don't want to be caught in this water at night."

It seemed we were in the water only seconds when Hoagy had his reel singing. "Rainbow on!" he cried out. I watched him fight his fish, a leaping rainbow of about five pounds. It made me think of the Battenkill and how hard we had to work for a strike; to hear your reel sing—that was rare!

"Come on, George," I heard Adrian's voice behind me. "We'll go below. Let Hoagy have fun on the *poza*. I know a good place for big browns, but we have to cross the river."

Cross this river? Where? How? This river was more like an ocean run, but I followed Adrian downstream along the rounded slippery stones.

Above us several black-faced ibises screamed harshly into the eternal evening sky. The sun was already low on its western passage and the peaks of the mountains glowed orange and pink.

37

"We'll cross here," said Adrian finally. "But you must follow ten yards behind me. If the current is too tough I'll turn back."

Then, picking up a strong wooden stick for me and another for himself, Adrian started to cross the river. I followed him deeper and deeper into the water, stabbing the rocks with my stick so that the current wouldn't twist my legs around and take me down. Several times Adrian stopped and rested and I did the same for the current was relentless.

Slowly we moved across the river, probing between the stones, pressing all our weight against the current. From rock to rock we inched forward, so slowly, until the water seemed to be dropping away from our boots and we were miraculously secure on a tail of rocky island in the middle of the turbulent Calcurrupe. My legs were trembling inside my boots. I felt as though I had just survived an impossible mountain climb, and I generously thanked Adrian for that precious stick, which I knew I would need again for the long journey back to shore.

"We don't have too much time to fish now," said Adrian. "Try my 'Cumilahue special' against those trout in the riffles. Let's move up a big one to bring back and show Hoagy!"

As I whipped out the fly over the riffles and danced it in across the surface, a little trout struck ferociously.

"Sardinas!" shouted Adrian. "There's a big one rising in the deeper channel. He's yours!"

I had seen him too, a fat rainbow of maybe ten or twelve pounds. Quickly, I dried the fly and let it sail above the big trout's watery den. In the waning light I could see the peacock feathers sparkling on the water and then they disappeared, suddenly, and the strike and the bent rod and the reel singing happened all at once and my monster rainbow was in the air flashing in the scarlet sun.

"You're into one of Calcurrupe's witches!" Adrian cried. "Hold her, she's going to give you a long fight."

Pounding down into the deep now with all her strength, the witch of the Calcurrupe began to run into the backing of my reel. I had never seen line go out so quickly and with such burning force. Up she came again, higher this time, and she was a beautiful witch!

I tried to reel in as much line as I could when she made her most spectacular jump, but she was meant to be with her river, wild and haunted, free.

"She's gone," my voice choked with failure.

"Leader give way?" Adrian asked sadly.

"Fisherman, fisherman gave way," I said, gazing down the endless darkening run.

Adrian fell silent with me for a moment. "You'll have to come back in the spring to find her again," he said. "She'll want to ride her broomstick for you once more."

I looked across river, aware that it was time to go back. Night was falling swiftly, and stars were lighting trails upon the sky.

"It's going to be tougher this time," Adrian cautioned as he reached down for our sticks. "I hope we won't have any trouble."

Now as you couldn't see where you were stepping or how deep the water was in front of you, you sensed the full terror of the river. Each step forward seemed to be taking you into greater unknown dangers.

"We've taken the wrong way!" cried Adrian with alarm.

"But it's too late—we can't turn around or we will be swept down. So that's it—we've got to keep moving!"

I could feel the current growing stronger, trying to pull my legs from under me. I told myself that I must not let that happen, or down the river I would go.

"Rest!" said Adrian, swaying in the water a yard or so in front of me.

The stick throbbed in my hand and for a moment, I believe the longest moment of my life, I looked down into the swirls of water and a strange calmness came over me. I wanted the river to take me. I wanted to run with the river anywhere it wanted to go.

"Don't look into the water!" Adrian shouted instinctively. "Look to the bank, to the trees, look into the stars, but not the water!"

Suddenly, I could feel water rushing over the tops of my chest waders, and I realized if I went down my favorite Payne would be lost forever, and I wasn't going to let the witch of the Calcurrupe take that from me. Now I was fighting the river with all my strength. I was no longer behind Adrian. I was coming up quickly alongside of him. I was going to reach that bank standing up with him.

When we pulled our aching bodies out of the Calcurrupe, Adrian began to laugh.

"Can you imagine," he drew a deep double breath, "can you imagine if cameras were set up to film one hundred fishermen trying to cross the Calcurrupe where we crossed it? How many would be left standing with their rods still in their hands!"

Later that evening we played chess and we drank wine and we weighed Hoagy's magnificent five-pound trout. But the conversation kept drifting back to the river crossing of the trail of witches. Trout fishing is more than just catching the trouts; it's coming close to something inside yourself, a clearing for your soul, a touch of time when you bring about the wheel of who you are.

When the Piper Cherokee lifted us into the sky I looked down upon the Calcurrupe like one of the stars I had seen in the sky that evening. I wondered if I would ever return to Llifén where the world ends. I wondered if my witch would be waiting for me, and there was a feeling inside me that something new was beginning and would last a long time.

Fishing with Hemingway in Spain

HEMINGWAY, worm-fisherman:

I got my rod that was leaning against the tree, took the bait-can and landing-net, and walked out onto the dam. It was built to provide a head of water for driving logs. The gate was up, and I sat on one of the squared timbers and watched the smooth apron of water before the river tumbled into the falls. In the white water at the foot of the dam it was deep. As I baited up, a trout shot up out of the white water into the falls and was carried down. Before I could finish baiting, another trout jumped at the falls, making the same lovely arc and disappearing into the water that was thundering down. I put on a good-sized sinker and dropped into the white water close to the edge of the timbers of the dam.

I did not feel the first trout strike. When I started to pull up I felt that I had one and brought him, fighting and bending the rod almost double, out of the boiling water at the foot of the falls, and swung him up and onto the dam. He was a good trout, and I banged his head against the timber so that he quivered out straight, and then slipped him into my bag.

—From *The Sun Also Rises*

So YOU THOUGHT the old man was dead, dreaming about the lions. Oh, no, pescadores! He lives in Spain, fishing the morning lonely on the Rio Tormes, a blue-green, mountain-cradled *rio* about three hours' drive west of Madrid. And as legends live, the brown-flowered trouts still come for his fly when the river-cooled wine has seen the last light of day and night comes like a stranger on the trail.

Hemingway's ghost lives not in Idaho or Cuba or in his books, but in the stream-swings of Gredos, and you can talk to him if he will allow you to interrupt his fishing moods. Or he will talk to you, yes, if you've been drinking with him, squirting Rioja's *Marques de Murrieta* from the goatskin to your lips. He will talk to you in whispers through the clear waters of the Tormes and recite the poetry of Machado through the wind-dappled leaves of the poplars by the banks.

> Al andar se hace camino
> Y al volver la vista atras
> Se ve la senda que nunca
> Se ha de volver a pisar
>
> As you walk, you make the road
> And, looking back,

When Charles Ritz viewed this photograph of me fishing the Rio Tormes in Spain he wrote on the back of the print: "Providing the back of the line is tied to a tree, the cast is perfect because the vertical wrist here is correct." The signature read: "Charles the fly-swatter"

In Madrid I had a pair of hunting boots made for me by Tenorio, the same *zapateria* who fitted Ernest Hemingway in 1956. Tenorio told me that Hemingway had a "truly gigantic bunion on his right foot," shown here on Tenorio's sketch, and special care had to be taken in shaping the boot.

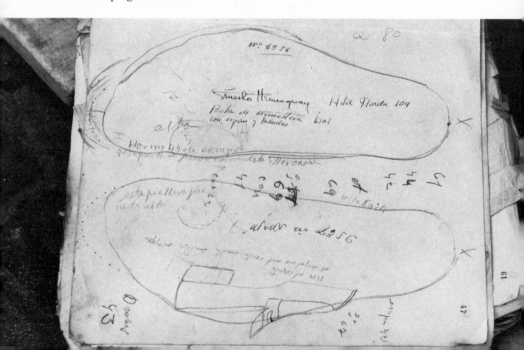

You see the path that you
Will never again have to walk

José Andrés Nuñez, river guard over all *cotos* on the Tormes, swears with mixed breath of wine, peasant bread and *manchego* that it is true—the old man has never left his river. He had guided Hemingway back in 1956 when the great lion was spending his days haunting the echoes of *Cuchilleros* and running with the bulls.

Hemingway had come to the Tormes with *caña para trucha, moscas de Leon* and hand-stitched hunting boots made for him by the master bootmaker Tenorio, in Madrid.

José said the old man fished with three flies-a-time and took many trouts, fat and as brown as the stones of the Tormes.

"He talked to the trouts with the poetry of Lorca and Machado," José exclaimed. "And the trouts always came to him and they were in a great hurry to do so."

"Reminds me of a rare fisherman on the Battenkill in Vermont," I said to José. "He talks to the trouts too, especially when the moon is down and the summer brown is stalking. This man I know is a quiet man, not as famous as Hemingway. His name is Soper, and he takes the trouts on one fly like Gary Cooper took *High Noon* with one gun strapped to his side."

José's eyes came up beaming. "Your friend, Soper—he drinks good too?"

"He's been known to run with the bulls," I answered. "And I believe him to be one of the best fishermen of trouts in the world—even though there are many who regard themselves as Hemingways of the stream!"

"He drinks then, for sure," José confirmed. "Next time you bring Soper, and Hemingway will talk to him by my river and we'll all drink from the *bota* and catch many *truchas!*"

"That would be a day, what a day!" I said, thinking for a moment about how long it had been since I had seen Dudley Soper. How many years now? It's been twelve years since he plucked those two magical wedding trout for Nicole. Remember—by the old Battenkill dam?

Over the years I had been traveling to all parts of the world in search of streams and trouts. Yet, there was Soper living in Delmar, New York, not a widely traveled man, but a man who instinctively knew more about the mysteries of the trouts than an army of self-proclaimed experts. Soper, a gentle man with nothing to prove, was born so, born to the poetry and delicacy of the meanings of the river.

Drink a glass of fog with the mist men on the Battenkill when the moon is down and they will tell you about Dudley Soper.

José poked inside a pocket of his corduroy jacket and, producing a few hand-tied scraggly looking flies, urged me to drop three on my leader the way his old friend had done. I thanked José but explained I felt more comfortable with one fly a-time, and, proudly, I showed him a little parachute, sulphur-bodied, that Soper had tied for me one Christmas a long time ago. José looked down at my single fly and shook his head as though he were deeply troubled. My wife, Nicole, sensing his disappointment, offered to try them at once. José smiled and quickly rigged up his *caña para trucha* for her, a sturdy, homemade rod with heavy cord wrapping the guides.

It was a wonderful March day, snow gleaming from the peaks of the Sierra de Gredos and the sun spilling warmer on your face as morning advanced to noon.

46

José Andres Nuñez, river guard of the
Tormes, taking me to the pools where
Hemingway had fished.

Trout began breaking across stream and rings appeared in the middle currents, and my heart surged. The trees on the opposite bank were softly reflected upon the water's surface, a lone eagle drifted on the wind overhead, a water rattler periscoped and then disappeared in the dark fingers of a tree's rivered-out roots.

As I made my way upstream with my eye on a nest of white-water rocks, I could not help but feel I was the luckiest man alive. And could you blame me? Here we were, Nicole and I, trout fishing together in Spain for two weeks. As guests of the Spanish government, we were being courted beyond belief: accommodations at the Ritz, a chauffeur ready to take us to any stream we decided to fish, all our expenses paid in the air, on the road, in Madrid and wherever we stayed in the country. We were living the dream of a lifetime!

Suddenly, my reverie was jarred when I heard Nicole cry out "Fish on!" Turning out of my thoughts, I saw Nicole with a trout. No, two trout—three? I had to go back to see what all the fuss was about. Yes, she had taken two trout on her cast of three flies-a-time just like *el Papa* had done. I couldn't believe my eyes! Nicole was laughing wildly. "If only Hoagy could see this!" she blurted wickedly.

"What about me?" I stammered. And here I was going upstream like Gary Cooper. "Perhaps I should try those flies, José."

"Oh no!" Nicole put up a firm hand. "You fish your old *purista* way and I'll fish José's way." José really liked that, and he took a long gulp from his *bota*.

I looked down at Nicole's two fine trout, each about a foot in length and with beautiful markings—yellow and red and the color of the Tormes stone on their backs.

Picnic time in Spain, a fisherman and his guide. In the glop of humanity a soul has to get lost and be by himself, where no words are spoken—only sounds from the river and wind in the flowers.

"It looks as though we're going to eat tonight!" I ventured with relish.

"Well, I know *we're* going to eat," Nicole replied winking at José. "I don't know what *you're* going to eat!"

After our noon picnic of wine and hot rabbit, *cabra* cheese and oranges and little pears, I had still not caught my first Tormes trout. But following a meal like that you did not expect to catch anything except a few hours' siesta, which is, after all, part of the Spanish way of life.

Do you know a better place in the world to make your bed than by a trout stream, your head resting against the pillow of a soft, grassy bank and the river full of whispers with the slow, quiet way of water leading your dreams on?

I sat up with a start, my eyes wide, searching upstream and round the shadowy bend of the Tormes. Had I heard something—a flash of sound from the river, and then gone.

"You hear him too?" José murmured as he gazed out toward the Tormes. "It means the fish must be moving."

That evening the *Parador Nacional de Gredos* presented us with two smoked trout, Nicole's catch for the day.

"Don't feel so bad," she said, "tomorrow is another day and besides, if you don't catch trout, there is still Spanish poetry you can hear from the Tormes."

In the days that followed the trouts were many and they were kind to me, not *grande,* but *pequeño,* and I found myself talking to the trouts and making up poems for them.

We fished with José from one coto to the next, and it always surprised him when I took a trout with my one lonely fly afloat in the currents of his river. As for voices from the river, I was so busy fishing and picnicking with Nicole and José that I

My wife, Nicole, captured this snow-winding scene as we were making our way to the Tormes. I remember lizards were sunbathing on the rocks that day and little Spanish flowers were singing their songs.

don't think I ever heard them again. Though I confess, certain Spanish passages seem to stick in my mind and one in particular keeps coming back, a flash of sound from the river:

> As you walk, you make the road
> And, looking back,
> You see the path that you
> Will never again have to walk . . .

For Charles Ritz,
from Yugoslavia

September Song.

Dear Charles,

I will be coming to Paris soon to visit you along the cool cobblestones of *Père Lachaise* for I have many stories to tell you about my fishing days in Yugoslavia, a country you had strongly recommended as an essential pilgrimage for my round-the-world fishing almanac.

I'll throw up my few bags in the petite chambre Numero 152 you always hold for me at the Ritz and, being a soft-hearted dreamer (I don't think there are many left), I'll want to look out below to the Vendôme garden where we used to talk for hours about lines and trout rods and places still left in the world where trouts and salmon wait for stream-hunters like us.

In my mind's eye I can still see you sipping your cold Perrier

53

and lemon slice under the shade of the ancient chestnut trees, geraniums and fern around us everywhere, and at the far end of the garden, a fountain in watery bloom. It was May, I remember, just before the terrible plaguelike heat fell upon most of Europe, scorching the land and drying out your favorite trout and grayling reaches.

We were talking about trout rods and you held one of my most cherished rods in your casting grip, my seven-and-one-half-foot Payne, an original. "A museum piece!" you had exclaimed vigorously. "Go to graphite!"

But then, observing my sudden depression, you conceded: "Payne was the master of them all!"

"What about Garrison?" I ventured with curiosity, since I possessed two fine Garrison sticks worth a pocketful of gold.

"A great technician," you confirmed. "But Payne was still the master, both an artist and a genius."

"Well, I shall call my museum the 'Museum of Bamboo Trout Rods for Technicians, Artists and Geniuses.'"

"Don't forget, 'fools.'"

"Perhaps all of us have become a bit too professional about this gentle pastime," I said, remembering that those were the words Norman Rockwell had used when I asked him if he had ever fished the Battenkill when he lived in Arlington, Vermont.

Too professional; something to think about. How can anyone not realize that he might take himself too seriously from time to time? How many fishermen approach the trout stream like surgeons ready to operate? How many fish merely to run against you; catch a bigger fish and you are magically a bigger man. Nonsense! Trout fishing is the flower of your soul, your unwritten poems, your freedom to be yourself.

I have flies stuffed away from all over the world. I think if
I used a different fly each day I could fish for a thousand
years. Now I have eighteen famous Gacka flies created
by Milan Stefanac. They work.

What impresses me most of life is what I don't know, what I have yet to discover; all those mysteries buried beneath rivers flung across the world. And oh, how vast and endless is my search to taste the sweet water as near and far away as I can find it running to the sea.

"Where are you going to fish next?" your words fell upon my dreams like a net, Charles.

"This book could go on forever," I said. "I hope it does."

"Have you fished Yugoslavia?"

"Yugoslavia! Trout in Yugoslavia?" I had not, as yet, explored that part of the world.

"You can't call yourself a fisherman, a true journey-fisherman of trouts until you fish the Gacka and the Sava Bohinjka and the Vintgar in one of my favorite countries to fish, Yugoslavia."

"I was planning to close my book with Afghanistan," I said.

"You will never close your book. You know that." Your eyes twinkled with vicarious joy. "There is still Africa and the Karnali in Kathmandu and Tierra del Fuego, and who knows where the streams are to be found in the afterworld."

Undeniably, Charles Ritz knew the truth: my search for streams was endless. In the past few years I had fished the best rivers in both North and South America, Canada and most of Europe.

And now my heart was saying, *Go to Yugoslavia, what are you waiting for fisherman?*

The sun was going down and shadows gathered in the Vendôme garden, shifting in restless pools. I remember how tired you looked, Charles. Would I ever see you again?

As you got up to leave I thought to myself, *Yes, I will go to Yugoslavia and I will fish there and I'll send you flowers from the banks of the Gacka and the Sava Bohinjka and the Vintgar,*

Fishing the Sava Bohinjka in Yugoslavia.
The water is ice-cold and filled with
fighting trouts. Yugoslavia is truly a
trout fisherman's dream.

*and my flowers will bring forth the sweetest memories for you,
of a time past, dear old friend.*

To reach the limestone and chalk streams of Yugoslavia is
an adventure in itself, an adventure of mountain peaks and
narrow roads twisting around mountains like coils of bark
round a tree, and of streams and rivers pulsing everywhere,
gushing and falling thunderously above.

On this romantic trip, Nicole and my five-year-old-son Ryan
were my fishing companions. Nicole came geared with more
cameras and lenses than I had packed rods and reels. Ryan, my
spirited, song-bird boy, would later enchant me with his songs
to the Gacka, gentle, fragrant little songs poured out of his
heart to that ox of water, the Gacka.

When we reached the Julian Alps I should have been exhausted, since I had been driving for almost twelve steady
hours. But the mountains and the crackling forest air were
exhilarating and, as we drove on into Bled, at the foot of the
Alps, I felt renewed. "I can smell the rivers and the trouts!" I
cried out to Nicole and Ryan. We had made it, Charles. We
were here ready to fish all the rivers you had told me about in
the Vendôme garden.

That same evening I could not resist booting up and fishing
the Vintgar, a pure, crystal-clear river, much colder at this time
of year than my beloved Battenkill, now running her lovely
midday course almost five thousand miles away.

It was July and sweltering throughout most of Europe, and
here we were larking in the cool of our first evening in Yugoslavia with trout-filled waters dancing in our heads.

On strange waters I always feel lucky. I feel as though I am
Gulliver walking mysterious streams. I tell myself every cast

Each cast should be perfect because it's
part of yourself; a cast is your spirit going
to the river as straight as your heart feels
it. Here am I, Charles, casting to your
Gacka.

must be a work of art, that I have come to the river invited by God.

On my early casts, I probed the secrets of the currents with my favorite selection of "Battenkillers," and in the draining hours of daylight several strong, marbled trout, running a pound, pound and a half, found my presentations irresistible. And when you hear your reel singing, do you know a sweeter song?

Ryan was on the bank humming to the river with his sweater pulled down to the knees of his jeans. Nicole was angling as she clicked each shot of her Nikon. And I was in my heaven wondering how big the trout would be under the lips of the dam in front of me—casting to it, waiting, watching the fly drift in the watery light. Before the fall of darkness, I changed over to a feathery Coachman, dressed it lightly with mucilin, and swooshed my line to the tongues of water spilling over the wooden dam. Suddenly, a fierce strike that stops a fisherman's heart; a flashing jump and my son crying like mad from the bank, "Daddy's got a big one! Look!"

She was a beautiful fish, as cold as the river, three pounds or more with soft coloring against her stoney grey sides, a treasure of a trout. But I did not kill her. I said to my fish: "I'll leave you for Charles."

That night the moon came full on Bled Lake in Slovenia. From our high balcony we could see across the lake to the island castle, a romantic relic of the Middle Ages. And in the distance the highest mountain, Triglav, rising into the night stars, her glaciated limestone and granite peaks appearing ghostlike under an illusory veil of fallen snow.

"I'm glad you came to Yugoslavia," I said to Nicole.

Concentrating on the rise! Pipe smokers
and fishermen on the Gacka in Yugoslavia. My companion is Doctor Zlatko,
Yugoslavia's premier trout fisherman.

"Are you glad I'm here too?" Ryan's voice reached us from the half-darkness of our room where he should have been sleeping.

Nicole smiled. "I think we're all happy to be here—it's like a dream, so far away from our world."

The next three days were spent exploring the streams of Bled, playing tennis in the early afternoon, and trying to get information from the one and only serious angler in town, a continental bartender at the elegant Toplice Hotel. He finally gave up his choice limestone pools along the Sava Bohinjka and Vintgar to one determined American angler.

Fishing the Sava Bohinjka was a gentle joy; I could see the trouts rising in the window-clear currents. The gravel-bottomed Sava Bohinjka was extremely slippery, and I soon found myself sliding along the stones to reach a casting station. But the fishing was excellent, and I was taking both rainbows and very dark brown trout over one pound on almost every second cast.

The flies that I found most effective for both the Sava Bohinjka and Vintgar were the compara-hatch flies George Schlotter of the Battenkill Anglers' Nook had tied up for me before our trip: Hendrickson, Grey Fox, Pale Evening Dun, Blue-Winged Olive, and Dun Variant.

I also tried several of your flies, Charles: Frank Sawyer's grey nymph and pheasant tail, and they worked well, fished naturally beneath the surface film—a tense line between your fingers and your rod high, ready for the sudden strike.

A few final impressions before leaving the Sava Bohinjka. You will find the trout fishing expensive, fifteen dollars for your daily pleasures by the stream; the food, basic and earthy, certainly not your favorite restaurant in Paris; the people in Slo-

In the fields men and women haying
while I work my flies.

venia, reserved and polite; the streams, lovely and wadeable at almost any point along the banks.

And, Charles, to prove the world grows smaller, I had encountered two "stream shoppers" from New Jersey who were looking for trout-fishing spots around the world so that they could package tours for American anglers. Ah, if only Thoreau had met them! One was patched with a new "Trout Unlimited" seal on his fishing vest while his companion, a woman, seemed to be his ferret for information. At lunch they asked me if I knew the difference between a limestone river and a chalk stream. How would you have answered such a question, Charles? Too professional.

An unforgettable experience of the trip was making the adventurous run from Bled to the Gacka, a three-hundred-mile drive south which takes a full day at the wheel, since the east-west roads were really intended for jeeps and farm tractors or, more realistically, for ox-drawn wagons. It seemed as though we drove and drove along those dusty, bumpy roads for hours going nowhere.

"Where is the Gacka?" I kept asking Nicole.

"I think the maps are wrong," she said. "We should have reached Plitvice National Park by now."

"You think the map-makers shortened the miles to keep the fishermen happy?"

"I think the fishermen lengthen the miles with their impatience to get into their boots," she winked.

At that moment a gorgeous black Bentley passed us at great speed, plastering our windshield with heavy showers of dust from the road. For an instant I caught sight of a bamboo rod leaning against the back seat.

"Well," I said, "we must be on the right cowpath. They don't look as though they're going to plough a field."

"Maybe it's Hoagy and W. C. Fields racing you to the stream."

A good laugh always eases the burden, Charles.

Hours later we reached the waterfalls of Plitvice and, full of thirst, we stopped by a natural spring and filled an empty Zilavka bottle with the most delicious spring water we had ever tasted in our lives. When you come to Yugoslavia you must also stop by that forest-darkened road round the lakes of Plitvice and drink the ice-cold water spilling out of the secret springs of the mountains.

"Fountain of youth!" I exclaimed, as I splashed my face and hands with the rare mineral water, a gift from the inner earth. "The great Gacka has to be near!"

But it took us another two hours winding through the spectacular waterfalls of Plitvice National Park before we reached the Gacka Hotel, settled in a grassy meadow by the banks of the river. And we were, once again, in time for the evening rise!

The Gacka is one of the most beautiful rivers in all the world. A chalk stream filled with an abundance of shrimps and snaillike worms, Gacka River flows quietly but with tremendous strength through the tall grasses and summer flowers of Croatia. Buttercups and forget-me-nots and poppies sprinkle the fields, and strange plum ivy bells I picked for you, Charles.

Here is a river of haunting dreams and brown trout and silvery rainbows as long as your arm.

Flowing wide and deep with blue-flowered watercress weaving in her shallows, the Gacka River is a Croatian miracle separating a farmer's crude stone house from his fields, separating his children and animals from the wolves and bears roaming the mountains in the distance. The Gacka sings along with the men and women as they gather the season's hay in the fields along the banks. The Gacka is a mirror for morning clouds a-sail and the moon's golden net in the flowing darkness.

And the Gacka is an old man, bent before his time, and his peasant wife ferrying small stacks of hay in a long, dugout canoe to the opposite side of the river, poling against the timeless currents with a smile saying welcome to a stranger fishing the morning lonely.

Though I try not to be an envious man, Charles, I stood for a long time watching the farmers in the fields by the river—men and women pitching up hay with their wooden, hand-hewn haying forks, and young girls, too, working and singing. I was moved by their spirit and song in a world grown spiritless. Could I not live as simply as one of these peasants?

I remember after fishing the Gacka one evening, a Croatian family invited us to share *kava* with them by the banks of the river. The woman's hands and face were lined and parched by the sun and her daily labors in the fields. She kept touching Nicole's velvety cheeks and the leaf-smooth hands of my son Ryan. To feel silky, cream-soft skin was rare for this woman of the earth, and you could see that her young daughter's hands were already beginning to show the same signs of hard work. I could feel her pure heart opening to me. She was a creature of the earth, an old woman of the sun and the stars and the mysterious God who made a fisherman wonder about himself and his soul and the meanings of being a man in a suspicious world.

We twist and turn in small corners, as Seferis said, trying to escape from ourselves. If only life were a straight line, how we would live it then! I would fish and write my poems in Patagonia, I would drink wine by the Gacka with my fishing friend, Doctor Zlatko, who lives in an ancient village nearby called Otacac. He is a man who loves to read Jack London and Steinbeck and Antoine de Saint-Exupéry and who will take you fishing if he likes your way. I would watch the fall of stars over the Sierra de Gredos where the gentle Rio Tormes flows. I would fish and write my poems into the days of my snow-hair and only the rivers would be called my home. I would want all my evening rises to be like the last time on the Gacka.

> We were five fishermen on the banks
> waiting for the river to rain with the rise.
> Sachio from Japan, Gunther from Frankfurt,
> Eugene Rauscher from Saint Ouen,
> and the flower picker, Milan Stefanac,
> who makes trails through the grasses
> grown taller than the five
> come for the hour of the rise.
>
> Now to cast our dreams
> on the hooks of feathery fallings.
> To set it straight,
> to let the line run strong,
> to pick a flower hiding
> from a time ago, dear old friend . . .

Test and Itchen Diary

I'VE been now all over the world touching the streams and wild places of the trouts. I've walked the cliffs and banks of the dreamlike Boulder River in Montana, and I've picked purple loosestrife along the Loue River in Franche-Comté. In a few weeks I will be flying to the Malleo, Quilquihue, and Chimehuin in Argentina.

When will the madness be gone? Glorious in visions, all my rivers are like my fingers, a part of me forever, and I am possessed by them. I've never broken a blind date with a river. And I keep going back as though haunted by the primal forest that shelters the eternal stream. Is there music over the river? Is there humor and contentment? Is there a reawakening of love? Yes, and if you gaze deep into the face reflected in the water you might see yourself as you were once, young and wandering free.

Friday, August 29

ARRIVED AT Sheriff House in the little town of Stockbridge, England, in the late afternoon after a frenetic two-hour drive from Heathrow. Got lost only twice. On wrong side of road too many times. Dead tired. But expected by the River Test to meet Dermot Wilson, the legendary trout master. I'm so excited to be here I take a headache as my companion. Coffee, freshly brewed, helps as I wait for Dermot's partner, Bobby Morrison, to pick me up and get me to the fishing on time.

Bobby arrives in an old Bentley stockpiled with rods, reels, boots, flies, fishing books, nets, mucilin, more flies, everywhere flies, beautiful hand-tied flies. And brandy.

Dermot Wilson fishing with a young blonde, about twenty, who has just landed a five-pound rainbow. I'm suddenly brought to life. The chalk stream is idyllic—filled with watercress and blue flowers, forget-me-nots.

"Where the hell were you?" shouts Dermot by way of introducing himself. "You were supposed to have been here yesterday!"

First day, evening rise, I take three rainbow, two browns, all of good size, all returned "for luck"—which means you're really after a big one, aren't you? Dinner at an old inn, thatched and beamed, with a fireplace and good English beer.

Return to Sheriff House about midnight. I fall off to sleep faster than I ever have before.

Saturday, August 30

FISHING the "Ginger Beer Stretch" on the Test with Dermot. This is my day. Before noon I take a three-pound, twelve-ounce brown, heavy belly, brilliant colors. Time—fifteen minutes. On my seven-

On the Test in England:

an action sequence captured by Dermot Wilson.

foot Garrison. Fly number 16—Grey Goose—that Charles Ritz had given me in Paris. Tied by Frank Sawyer.

Fish Test at Kimbridge through the day into evening rise, return a three-pound rainbow and several sixteen-inch rainbows, all solid fighters.

After fishing we all sit down near an old cedar fishing hut by the stream and have a drink—Scotch and cold apple cider. In the distance I can see the Salisbury to Southampton train. Lights from Southampton glow in the night sky as though there is a world on fire somewhere.

We talk a while, drink, light our pipes; Dermot smokes his filters; and the evening drenches us with its beauty and solitude. One of the most memorable of all my fishing days and nights closes.

At Sheriff House I have a delicious lobster freshly caught from the North Sea, Meursault wine, and coffee—what coffee! Then a bath in a deep, long tub, and I fall asleep with the music of the chalk stream in my head.

Sunday, August 31

FOR BREAKFAST I have half my trout—a feast for a king, and I'm the king! Confess I sent the skeleton to a man I know who fishes like he plays golf with a message: "For Hoagy. It's all in the presentation."

Jack Sheppard, a man who knows a river from the bottom up, takes me to his prize—Chilbolton on the Test. It's paradise, friends of rod and line! Fishing from the banks of Disraeli's Elizabethan manor, I can see lawns rolling on like rugs; enormous trees everywhere, hanging beech, hawthorne, and one exotic giant brought to England as a seed from the Boxer War. Along the stream plum-colored orchids are growing about four inches high. Under the pines are nettles like the ones the Romans used for thrashing themselves to improve circulation. A variety of wild ducks shares the river with me, coots, water hens or moor hens, grebe or mud hens.

I took four grayling on this cool, misty day; no hatch to speak of so I took a snooze at the fishing hut.

Learned from Jack Sheppard the names of the six greatest trout fishermen: Dermot Wilson; Frank Sawyer of the Nether Avon; Reg Righini, Yorkshire man, grayling and Atlantic salmon expert; Raymond Rocher of France, an English professor; Charles Ritz; an American "cocksman" and braggart.

At Chilbolton on the Test, I saw grayling, rainbow, big browns, salmon and one enormous pike that infuriated Jack Sheppard: "I'm going to hit that ———— on the nose with a hard lure and sock him the hell out of my river!" I had no doubt that the old pike saw the bushes before the fall of night.

Monday, September 1

At Kimbridge on the Test with Dermot Wilson. I took four rainbows, twelve to eighteen inches. One brown about seven pounds.

Again, sticking mostly to Frank Sawyer's deadly Grey Goose.

Spent good part of the day talking with Dermot. Here are a few of Dermot Wilson's Wisdoms:

"I measure the cast, cover the cast, and then with luck, the fish is risen, hooked, played and landed.

"If I cover a Test trout with a reasonable representation of a fly he is feeding on, I'm surprised if he doesn't take it. If I cover an Itchen trout with a perfect representation of a fly he is feeding on, I'm surprised if he does take it.

"On a gloomy day I would just as soon sit and watch. I know the fish can be taken.

"Itchen trout have been successful adversaries for so long that I fish obsessively for them."

Dermot informed me that the best time to fish the Itchen is May

73

through early June and the first two weeks in October.

In my notebook of flowers I place rosebay willow herb, purple loosestrife, forget-me-nots, yellow flag, ranunculus or water buttercups. Yellow musk and mimulus grow wild along the Itchen and the Test.

Tuesday, September 2

FISHING THE Itchen at Abbotts Worthy with His Grace, Len Bishop. Trout are elusive on the "Fulling Stretch." I watch as His Grace takes one. His Grace watches me as I take none.

Wednesday, September 3

FINALLY I'M ready to set off into the world again; before dawn cracks I'm on the road back to Paris. Goodbye Stockbridge, Dermot, Jack and Bobby; your chalk streams and your flowers and your Salisbury to Southampton train will be part of me forever.

BORD FÁILTE ÉIREANN   Irish Tourist Board

Baggot Street Bridge, Dublin 2

Telephone : Dublin 765871
Telegrams : Fáilte, Dublin
Telex   : Dublin 5367

Mr George Mendoza
c/o Ashford Castle Hotel
Cong
Co Mayo

14 May 1976

<u>TO WHOM IT MAY CONCERN</u>

This is to certify that Mr George Mendoza has engaged in honest fishing for
brown trout in the beautiful lakes of western Ireland, and that, to the best
of my knowledge, he has not up to this point in time, told lies about the size,
weight, or number he has caught.

Eamonn Ceannt
Director General

Trout fishing is my romance with life being born over and over again. It's the greatest escape I know from the world. To fish for trouts I've slept in broken-down inns, cabins with wood stoves, a Vermont house about to fall into the

Battenkill, *hosterias*, tents set up in the pine woods, even in my old Mercedes-Benz. If I could I would make the river my bed. Here I am in County Mayo, Ireland, ready to fish out the dreams of my half-Irish heart.

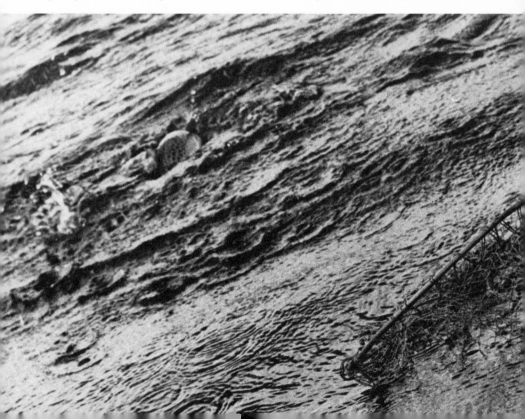

Your hand on the cork, your reel over rising trouts, your fingers trigger
Is there not a magic in all of this, a poem? Don't ask me. I'm never ho

Fly Fishing for Trophy Tuna

*W*HEN I boarded *Alcor III* tied up in her berth at Punta de Puerto Rico, Grand Canary Islands, Captain Antonio Deniz looked at my eight-foot, nine-inch graphite salmon fly rod weighing only four ounces, and he smiled.

"*Mucha suerte!*" he said, shaking his sun-marked, dark Spanish face from side to side. "The sea is very deep with fish out there so big they can tear a man's arm away."

"It will be a challenge," I said, looking around at the massive sea rods and reels resting on the weathered planks of the deck floor and strapped under the cabin roof.

"We are not fishing for *truchas*," he said. "If you hook a large tuna your rod might explode!" And then touching the rod and the Magnalite Multiplier reel as though they were made of feathers, he smiled again.

"I hope you are not expecting too much," he said. "The sea is often generous with her fishes, but only for those who can hold them."

It was almost eight o'clock in the morning. The docks were beginning to fill with people come mostly from Germany and the Netherlands to fish for a day in the sea between the Spanish archipelago in the Atlantic and the coast of southern Morocco.

Boats and their captains waited for fishing parties to board, and then engines coughed up gasoline and oil fumes and, one by one, the boats maneuvered out of their slips to the open sea.

It was a beautifully clear January day with a growing sea breeze sweeping across the snow peaks of Santa Cruz de Tenerife, which stood in the clouds to the west. As the *Alcor III* churned slowly through the oncoming swells, I noticed that the fishermen seated aft were already beginning to gulp down bottles of cold *cerveza*.

In the shelter of the cabin, I sipped a half cup of black coffee thinking about the adventurous drive I had made over the mountains of Gran Canaria the day before.

Up in the mountains the almond blossoms were rushing into bloom, pink and white and the color of plum deep inside their petals, and the cool mountain air was filled with an exotic fragrance no bottle ever held.

That is where to be, I thought, *up there in the mountains under the almond blossoms where the Spanish people live in small clusters of narrow winding villages or in caves carved out of the earth.*

Below the mountains were the beaches and the lavish hotels of Playa de Maspalomas and the tourists seeking soft drinks under the sun. I wondered how many got to the almond blossoms to feel the quick cold of the cliff winds on the crude road to Cruz de Tejeda. How many stood on the mountain lookout above all the villages and the hills and the sea to know what they came looking for?

Captain Deniz motioned for me to look ahead off the starboard bow. Turning quickly, I saw several fast moving tuna skiffs painted red and blue against the shimmering green of the Spanish sea.

Waving to the fishermen in the skiffs, Antonio suddenly brought our boat to full running speed to catch up with them.

"We'll pick up herring and mackerel from them," he said. "You may use only flies but the others will want fresh bait to long line shark and perhaps a giant tuna later on."

As Antonio pulled alongside the skiffs to take on fresh bait, I observed him closely as he chatted for a while with the men rolling close to the sea. It struck me that he must have done this a thousand times over the years going out to the fishing grounds; these men were his friends, his daily source of information, his point of communication with others who worked the sea.

When we pulled away, Antonio looked at me and said: "You may have your chance today. The tuna are up and moving, *grande, grande!*" He ordered his mate to let the lines out.

When I stepped to the stern to begin fishing with my Orvis salmon rod and reel, I could not help but feel a little self-conscious among the beer-happy, fish-hungry party of Germans. Here they were gripping heavy duty sea rods with reels as wide as your outstretched fingers. There I was with my twig-like rod, my number ten line attached to knotted sections of salmon leader and my flaming red bucktail, half the size of their lures, trailing astern as the *Alcor III* rode full throttle through the sea.

GRAN CANARIA, ESPAÑA
(SPAIN)

THIS IS TO CERTIFY THAT MR. GEORGE MENDOZA, AMERICAN

ANGLER-AUTHOR CAUGHT OFF THE COAST OF PUERTO RICO, GRAN

CANARIA, SPAIN, THE FOLLOWING FISH:

        SPECIES: TUNA (SKIPJACK)

        WEIGHT: 7 KILOS (15.4 lbs.)

        DATE CAUGHT: 17 JANUARY 1977

        TACKLE: 4 OUNCES SALMON FLY ROD, 6X LEADER

        BOAT: "ALCOR III"

        NAME OF CAPTAIN: ANTONIO DENIZ

        NAME OF OWNER: HAROLD MAGOVSKY,
                   PRESIDENT, "MAHAR, S.L."

THIS CATCH, TO THE BEST OF MY KNOWLEDGE AND BELIEF

CONSTITUTES A WORLD RECORD.

SIGNED IN PUERTO RICO, GRAN CANARIA, ESPANA, 12 MARCH, 1977.

ANTONIO DENIZ, CAPTAIN   HAROLD MAGOVSKY, PRESIDENT
M/Y "ALCOR III"   MAHAR, S.L.

How ridiculous, I thought. *What a sight I must be to these hunters!* Frequently, Antonio's mate urged me to take in more line so that I would not foul the other rigs.

I was beginning to feel crowded. *Too many lines out,* I thought, *too many fishermen trying to fish at the same time.* It was not being alone with a stretch of trout river you love, it was not the mountains and the almond trees, it was the tourist traps of Las Palmas and Playa de Maspalomas.

Suddenly, one of the Germans had a strike, a small albacore. Then a tuna around twelve pounds hit another lure and there was a lot of shouting, but the fish were reeled up quickly without a great fight and then hauled aboard by the mate's slashing hook.

I felt disgusted at the sight of blood washing the floorboards. Why not a net? But then I realized we were not fishing in a gentle trout stream, this was the sea of the awesome shark and the swordfish and the blue marlin that Hemingway hunted in his days off Cuba.

And then my fantasy of fishing in the ocean with a fly rod became even more absurd. What had I come across an ocean looking for?

Toward noon Antonio pulled up to a sea mooring where we had lunch. The mate set up heavier rods for the Germans to give them a chance at the monsters cruising the bottom. He baited massive hooks with one pound mackerels and globs of herring and dropped them over the side.

As the rays of the sun spiraled down on us, a man-sized blue shark surfaced to feed on discarded pieces of lunch.

"We are fishing for him," said Antonio, "and there he is wanting to eat us."

"It is a character trait among men too," I said.

"Did you know that the blue shark urinates through the skin and the gills?" said Antonio. "Some boats serve them for lunch. What a stink when they're soaking in salt water before being cooked! But the people don't know. They eat it and think it's a delicacy."

After several hours of fruitless fishing, Antonio got underway again. One of the Germans held up a six-inch shark; apparently he was going to save it as a souvenir. The balance of the *Alcor III*'s noon catch: a moray eel, several small albacore, and a baby octopus.

Once more I had my bucktail riding the golden wash of waves astern. I had the feeling that Antonio wanted me to catch a fish. I don't know why, but I think he liked me. I did not fish merely to kill and he knew that.

When my fish struck I saw it first. About seventy-five yards off, a great circle of spray rose in the sun. The mate shouted for Antonio to stop the boat, but by that time most of my line was stripped from the reel.

Antonio was so shocked that he just stared at me. He knew that I had hooked an important fish.

"Reverse her!" I yelled to Antonio. "I have no more line left."

Antonio threw the boat into reverse, and as the boat followed after the fish, I reeled in as fast as I could. I had to get a few hundred yards of backing on that reel again.

When we were almost upon the running fish, the mate cried, "It's a skipjack, *grande*!"

"Good God!" I gasped as the fish lurched away from me and

sounded. There was nothing I could do but let her run. She was like a boulder sinking on the end of my line.

Now the other fishermen were told to take in their rigs so that they would not foul my line. How fascinated they were to see my rod bending and my reel singing and soon they were cheering me on as I struggled against the fish.

I could see smoke coming from my reel. Was it possible? The grease was actually burning off the gears as line ripped through the guides in violent spurts.

"You're going to catch fire!" said Antonio, a big grin wrinkling his face.

"She's a witch," I said. "I don't know how long I can hold her. She keeps going down. I can't stop her."

"I can chase after her when she is on top," said Antonio, "but I can't go down after her."

I looked at my reel and saw that once again most of my backing was gone. What was I going to do? I didn't want to lose her, not now. The challenge was all there and I wanted to get her in, I wanted to see her.

When I tried to resist her by palming the reel to save what was left of my backing, she ran from me with all her sea strength, going deeper. For a moment I imagined the graphite exploding and the reel disintegrating in my hands. How much more could the rod take? I shuddered to think if I were fishing one of my favorite bamboo rods.

I've got to let her know I am stronger, I thought, *or she will win the battle.* She has kept it up for nearly an hour and so far I have been following her. The moment has come to change that.

My hands and arms felt sore, almost numb. I began to reel

86

in slowly, very slowly. She pulled back but this time I held her and did not give line. If I could get the backing, all of it, onto the reel, I was home.

It seemed eternity passed before I saw the main body of my fly line wrap securely once, twice, three times around the reel, and as I kept winding in I felt the unseen strength of the fish ebbing. I told myself it was over, she was coming in. There was no reason to doubt the leader.

When she came up behind the boat I could hear her last heaving splash and then, suddenly, I saw the gaff raised, slashing down on her back. I cried out to stop, but it was too late.

Streaked with blood along her sides, she gleamed blue and green under the mellowing sun. I felt sorry for her. I felt I would never again fish in the sea.

Then I remember Antonio by my side, holding up the tippet of leader that still clung to the fly. He was very excited and kept shouting, *"Imposible! Imposible!"* He could not believe that six-pound test could hold sixteen pounds of fighting skipjack tuna.

I could not believe that I had forgotten to change my leader over to extra heavy eighteen-pound test for fishing in the Spanish sea.

Suffer Me, O Lord, to Catch a Fish

ONE evening a few summers ago, after trying to catch big browns for an *American Sportsman* film on the Boulder River in Montana, Slim Pickens and I fell dejected and exhausted by a campfire near the river's edge.

Guitar pluckings and wine and flickering birch logs in the fire softened our spirits, and we began to laugh again. Trout fishing is supposed to set you free from the worries of the world, but it can also tighten a man up inside. I admit it; sometimes I walk away from a river feeling like a stone not a flower. But there was pressure on us to catch a monster brown on delicate flies and we were not producing for our producer and director, Bud Morgan, one gentle man away from the camera.

"You were to teach me how, George," Slim drawled.

"I'm still learning myself, Slim."

"We all better learn pretty quick if we want to get a show on air!" Bud Morgan's words made everyone laugh, except Bud Morgan.

"Ah, shucks," said Slim, "we'll do it, heck I'll do it. There are many ways to catch a trout, you know."

"I hope you're still thinking of using those flies I gave you," said John Kirby, our guide along the Boulder River.

"Flies! By gosh, let me tell you a story about catching fish!

"You know, a number of years ago, I was fishing up there on the New Fork in Wyoming. Out of Pine Dale, Wyoming. Back up in that country that ole Jim Bridger and them mountain men run in. There was one stretch of that water there, where there was a bunch of brown trout that—I mean you never seen such big trout as these ole fish were. You'd go down there and take anything that they'd hit that was, you know, small enough that they'd hit the doggone thing, straighten the hook out and go on. There was just no doggone way you could hold 'em. I thought, 'Man, there's gotta be a way, by golly, that a guy can catch one of them big fish.' So one morning I decided I'd take a run down there on the New Fork and see what I could do. It was cold as anything. And I'd stopped by the Cowboy Barn. The ole boy that runs the thing says, 'Hey, somebody brought me a little bottle of moonshine in here.' And he says, 'It's pretty stout. Would you like to try it?' I took a shot of it. Man, it was stout. I mean, it was really stout. I says, 'What you gonna do with it?' He says, 'You can have it if you want it. It's too dog-gone rough for me.' And I said, 'It might look pretty good out there on the New Fork.' So I took that bottle and went on out there.

"I had some lures that I picked up down there at the Wind

Fishing for the *American Sportsman*, starring Slim Pickens and George Mendoza. To fish for trouts—and to be filmed while you're doing it— might make some twitch with envy!

River Sporting Goods and I figured, by golly, they might be able to handle one of them fish. So I got down there on the river, and with my spinning outfit I started working that water. Shoot, I ain't made but about three casts and *wham* I had one hit. And shoot, it never even slowed him up. I brought the lure on in, and there's that ole hook just straightened out. So I sat down and I had a little drink out of my bottle, tied on another lure and, by golly, I made four or five casts out there and man, I hooked another one and this time it took the lure and everything.

"Well, I sat down and had another drink and 'bout, I guess it must have been 'bout eleven o'clock, I'm out of lures and I ain't caught a fish. Them damn fish is running off with all my tackle. So I'm going around through that doggone tackle box and I found a great big old hook in there. Must have been a catfish hook or something like that. Was 'bout an inch and a half long and a big tough looking son-of-a-gun. I thought, 'Now if I just had something on that thing.' So I was sitting there looking at that hook and I killed the bottle. About that time a grasshopper jumped off out there and I thought, 'That's what I'll get.' So I took my bottle, and by golly, I started after some grasshoppers. And this big ole grasshopper, must have been 'bout an inch and a half, two inches long. Those big ole Wyoming grasshoppers, I caught and stuck seven or eight of them darn ole hoppers down in that bottle and they'd fall down in there and there's still a little bit of them ole moonshine doggone fumes in that bottle and it sure did get 'em pretty groggy right off the back, you know. And I'd catch some more and drop them right down there and put the cap on her.

"Finally I thought, 'Well, I've got enough to least start it anyhow,' so I went back and I tied this old hook on and I fished

out one of them ole grasshoppers out of the bottle. And I'm telling you. He was feeling no pain. And I threaded him on that
doggone hook, put a little weight on it, and, man, I popped the
thing out there—got it off out there, and had to have a little
weight to get him out there. And he sunk and went on drifting
on down and he hadn't drifted ten feet and *wham!* Boy, something hit. And this time it didn't give. And by golly, this ole
fish took off down the river and he's peeling that line off, by
golly, like there's no tomorrow, and I'm a-stumbling over these
rocks and trying to keep up with him and finally I'm in the
water pretty near up to my waist, going across places and trying
to keep him out of the brush and everything. And this fish just
keeps going on, and I must have went, oh, a quarter of a mile
down the doggone river and finally come to a place where it
kinda flattened out and there was a sand bar off out there and
by this time this ole fish is getting kinda tired and so was I. And
I worked around there and got him stopped and this doggone
thing, and finally eased him off out in this doggone place.

"By this time he's giving up pretty good and he rolled over on
his side and I got up to him and reached down and run a finger
in his gill and picked him up. And when I did I saw there was
something funny and I looked a little closer and I ain't even got
him hooked. By golly, this doggone grasshopper, this ole drunk
grasshopper had just grabbed him right by the throat and was
hanging on. Well, by golly, I just took him out and knocked
him over on the doggone head and took him—and that was the
first big trout. He weighed twenty-six pounds. This brown did.
That's the biggest trout that was caught all that season. By golly,
up there on the New Fork. I hope you believe that 'cause every-
body knows I'm very truthful."

The Last Garrison

I'M hiding out in the mountains with the last rod Garrison made. His friend, Hoagy, made certain that the words were heard: "George Mendoza got the last stick!" Now I appear gloriously holding my seven-foot Garrison on wanted posters alongside rivers and streams as though I'm some kind of legendary gunfighter.

I know that rare bamboo trout rods can touch a man's life forever: in the wood there is the magical return to your boyhood yearnings, in the wood there is your wish fulfilled—the perfect stick! But I never had any idea that buying the last rod of a great craftsman, actually completed by his hands, would incite gentlemen fishers of trouts to frenzy and madness.

A night ago I had to run from two men, one I thought I recognized as the Draculean wiry Italian who makes peeping music in the woods. Sounds like—*to be . . . to be . . . me . . . free*—sounds like spring frogs peeping. He, more than any fisherman I know, would do anything to possess my precious, golden fishing rod.

I had to fight my way through the darkening woods to reach my mountain cave. Oh that my life should be shaped like this, running and hiding, hunted and tracked, not knowing who is going to fall upon my path next, all for the last wood Garrison's hands sculpted.

Or perhaps I am caught in the web of madness, my brain spinning out fantasies?

Tonight, in the dark of my cave, the rod gleams, burns like gold in my eyes. What fire flames the stick? What makes the trout rise so when I raise it over the river? And when the wind blows the rod becomes a flute and pinches of sparrows flick round my head and whistle with the wood.

Garrison himself had wondered about the stick. Hoagy had brought him down to the old pink house by the river, and we struck up the rod there. Back and forth we played it, trying to balance silk with wood.

Hoagy said, "Four line sweet," and I felt five flowing through spirits. All the while Garrison stood back, watching in his gentle way that cared that a man and his fishing whip went together like the creating of the wood itself.

"Strong tips!" said Garrison, as though he doubted the rest. "Try it on the river, test it, make sure it's for you, it's got to be right for you." And then he said, "But if you take it, fish it, fish it hard, use it—don't buy it for *it to possess you!*"

Garrison came down to the river with Hoagy the next morning and we fished, and I caught him, now and then, casting an

Part of my collection, a Leonard, two Garrisons and a rare Payne. Will there be streams in the future for my son to use them?

eye in my direction, watching the wood as my line sailed to the lips of the river. I thought to myself: *He is weighing his work over and over in his mind, the way a poet throws his words to the stars hoping they'll seed somewhere beyond what he can see.*

I bought the rod, but it was more, much more than just for the piece of wood. It was in the meanings of many things all taken into me. It was the moment standing with a man royal, it was in the mirror of being on a boyhood trail once again, river trail of moss and rocks and the swirlings of secret fish and whispering mountains going up, forever up, and the river still winding on through the summer hills when night told a wanderer go home.

I can hear voices near the cave now—mumbles, the sound of leaves pressing close.

"Came this way."

"Gotta get that rod—gotta get that rod tonight."

Voices sounds familiar. Not the Italian. But who? I'll have to find another cave come morning. Higher up in the mountains.

"Not leaving till I get that rod."

That voice, yes, I know it. Hoagy! Hoagy too!

I'm moving up the mountain night, up to where snow streams race beneath the sun. I'm going up to see Mr. Garrison, for I've heard that the trout streams of Chile run through heaven as blue and white as God's dreams and that only golden rods with strong tips are selected there for fishing with all the fishing saints.

There's No Ending

In another month the Rio Tormes will be flowing full. The river guard says the river will reach my *mirador* and the fishing will be at its peak.

Observations Through
a River Gate

I HAVE fished for trouts and salmon with some
of the most remarkable trout fishermen in the
world: Adrian Dufflocq from Chile, Douglas Reid from Argentina, Dermot Wilson and Frank Sawyer from England,
Doctor Zlatko from Yugoslavia, Charles Ritz from France,
Michael Ryan from Ireland, Alfredo Pickman Urquijo from
Madrid, Odd Haraldsen from Norway, Dudley Soper and
Frank Mele from New York State. There are many others, but
I have observed, particularly of these fishermen, that they are
quiet men who love the ways of a river and give no time to
petty chatter. They love a good glass of wine, a touch of music,
and the lovely graces of a young girl's way.

After years traveling around the world and fishing for the
salmon and trouts I have discovered that most fishermen are

highly competitive, always proving to others how much they know and bragging about bringing a poor river to its knees—how they try to crush all they touch.

And now I've come to wonder if the catching of a trout or killing of a salmon represents for some fishermen, like Schwiebert and his followers, a form of sexual conquest to be played out over and over again, then to be sported with in the pages of self-important fishing journals.

I am aware with great sorrow that an abundance of ape-men, not gentle fishermen, exist along the stream. I am aware that there is an ugly, narrow side of many fishermen, but then is this not true of all men? Wouldn't you rather spend your time fishing the morning lonely than trying to alter the direction of the world?

Besides, as my good friend and fisher-of-the-sea Michael Fayer often warns over a pipe and drink: "Time is running away, George, and soon there will be no rivers and streams to fish. Get to your dreams now, before it's too late." I think about Michael's prophetic words every day of my life, and that's my reason for doing it now—you dream it, you do it!

I dream of rivers and poetry and so I am always running away, an escapist from the mechanical, sunless canyons of life where politicians and morbid souls concerned only with money and power choke off the young. In man's world injustice is king. Cities are graveyards of dreams, the drawings of children become old and real too soon. Remember how they first appeared—Picasso's cow or Klee's cat thinking of a bird?

The killing of innocence comes soon through teachers and television. We are all like bats in a cave swirling in darkness, screaming at each other, afraid to move into the light of new adventures.

I still find innocence in rivers, because rivers make their own paths under the gliders of wind and stars. Sometimes I sit close beside a river and listen to it, listen to it all night, until the sound of water rushing over rocks takes me far away.

Man has yet to live with nature the way the Indian did, standing before the plain, understanding the meanings of the universe: simple and giving, unselfish. Modern man wails and doubts even Christ! Modern man is a garbage dump of too many ideas floating around created for his green temples. Within his own soul he rots, bloated with greed and progress, and finally, the end-game, envy.

I am like the eagle soaring alone. Below in the fields

> the crows assemble and squawk at each other
> for mysterious reasons.
> Up winds along the cliff-side
> suddenly take me higher
> into the branches of sun arrows.
>
> I feel free here all alone,
> my wing feathers whistling.
> I will stay up here, eyes sharp
> on my river running
> bursts of silver through the mountain gorge.

I will be my own man dreaming to the end where I will find my beginnings.

Butterfly under Mountain

IN front of me the mountain grows up, a lion's
head of fossil stone faces away from the sun. The
mountain is like a huge rock pillow against the sky. If the
mountain had a voice it would say

> rest against me stranger,
> wait with me till night falls
> and stars come beaming
> and Venus mound of light
> pours us a glass of wild dandelion wine.

I'm looking at the mountain and thinking many things; my
head is a net for memories and thoughts and dreams, all coming
and going like fish in the sea. I don't wish to hold anything
long. I never did, except for the rare moments of life—like the

morning of this day that began cool, and the noon of this day filled with a Montana river and rainbows dancing down the falls of the canyon, and this evening, honey-glow evening, that will be coming by soon now, looking for a fishing friend.

I am a bum. I am under the river and under the sea and there is the mountain and I am under the mountain, a butterfly lighting the flowers, flaming the fields.

I have no path and no stars guide me home. I am a blade of grass taller than a mountain. I am at my best when I'm in my boots on the brook and both ways upstream and downstream are empty of people and the traffic of sounds from the cities. I am the fallen leaf of October yellow and the wildness of weeds and grasses growing together out of the same earth.

I am a bum. And I am a poet. I am a notebook of dreams that opens without words and goes on without words for the word has come to be a vacant husk and I would rather we could speak without the use of words for they are meaningless and full of false weights.

Oh, let us put our dreams into the air and let them go like the time before when we were children and not so mixed into the ways of the world.

Walk with me into the night high up into the mountain wind. The trail is dark, no street lamps to secure our feet. The stars are distant. I've never felt they were friendly only far away like where you began and where you think home is and the voice of someone you tried to love.

Darkness is in the wind and it comes down upon the world filling it like a tide and we become fish once more and so we sleep under our ledges while dreams move into us creeping with fog.

And now, after all this, what have we understood? Who can answer? A grasshopper rattles and flies. There is something to learn from an inconsequential creature. Perhaps that it lives, keeps coming back, tunes the fields, lights the flowers, flames the fields.

Listen to me
you who cross this path:
I am buried here—
in everything of everything
in the earth of the earth
and in the wood of the tree
and in the waters of every stream
and in the leaves of all leaves
along the ivy-falling brook
and in the low meadows
where the stars graze on sleep
in everything I am
more, O more, than stone and words on stone
remind the coffined earth
a man's bones beneath lie.

Fragments from
a Notebook

I ONCE asked the playwright, Samuel Beckett,
why he felt words and writings were so empty
for him now. His reply: "If I could tell you, I wouldn't—but
I'd grow silent and young with you by your stream."

> "Sir, but that Angling is an art,
> and an art worth your learning:
> the question is rather, whether
> you be capable of learning it?
> for Angling is somewhat like
> Poetry,
> men are to be born so:
> I mean with inclination to it,
> though both may be heightened
> by discourse and practice;

but he that hopes to be
a good Angler must not only
bring an inquiring, searching,
observing wit, but he must bring
a large measure of hope and patience,
and a love and propensity to the art
itself;
but having once got and practised it,
then doubt not but Angling will prove
to be so pleasant, that it will prove
to be like virtue,
a reward to itself . . ."

—*Piscator*, Izaak Walton

Ready for lunch, dolly varden, salmon, and a crab—Rivers Inlet,
British Columbia.

The author trying to reach salmon breaking in the surf, Rivers Inlet,
British Columbia.

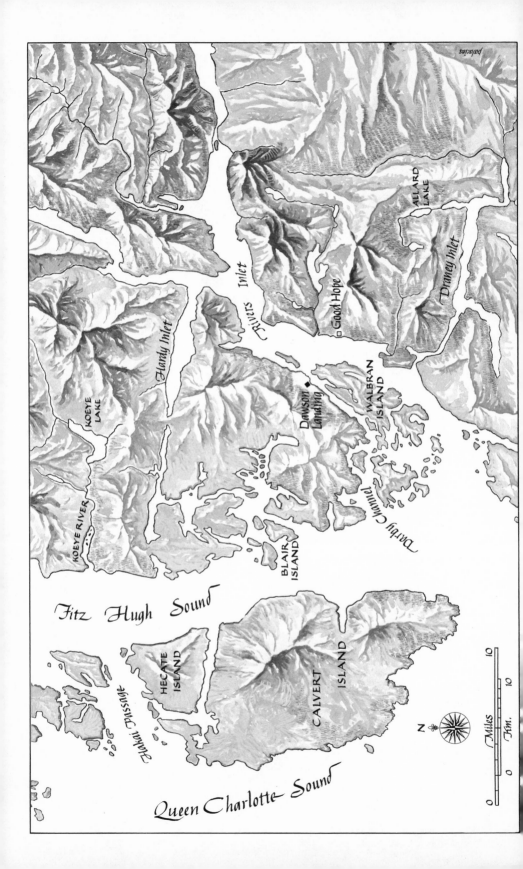

Looking at this map of rivers and high mountain lakes filled with salmon and native trout is like looking into a mirror of of memories. Here is that man-removed part of British Columbia that my heart stakes out for its own. There is the Good Hope Cannery Lodge standing over Rivers Inlet where you eat and sleep and listen to Bach under the stars while the rhythm of God Henry's tide pulses through you. There is Allard Lake one mile up the pathless mountain through the forest of fresh grizzly tracks where you caught wild cutthroats almost till dark.

There is Darby Channel and the Hakai Passage to the Pacific and the sandy mouth of the Koeye River where you took your first, most beautiful salmon under the green filtered mist of morning fog.

A map is in the veins of your eye, if it's where you want to be. My maps are many and they tell stories back to me like the moon's golden running on rivers as far away as your dreams.

Rio Tormes, stepping down while an
empty guardhouse keeps watch.

There's No Ending

*A*LL my life I've been giving over to a way out of this world. I've always believed that the path of escape was a winding road of rocks with water running wild and beneath, jewels of fish as mysterious as life itself. What does a river mean to a man? What comes into his head when the river is near? What are his dreams?

A pure fisherman is a poet, full of beauty and flight. He knows the names of flowers that grow along the stream, and he speaks to the waxwings in the branches above. He fishes the river not to catch the trouts but to become one with his soul and his God. A pure fisherman reads and remembers poetry. He dreams of one day fishing in the mountains of Andorra or among the flowers of Asturias.

Most fishermen I have known are quite boring and oddly

overweight. They are too preoccupied with their acquired knowledge of the sport and what clubs they belong to, and behold their fancy gear!

No, this is not the pure fisherman. This is a hunter, a man who wants to run against you, a man who has missed the meanings of the river.

> And so the boy still walks in me
> as he wandered long ago
> on a Vermont brook
> when the boy discovered
> the world had a beginning . . .
> and in the trees
> the wind made songs
> and the leaves were like
> the lips of a child . . .
> And in the boy
> there is no ending
> as the man watches him
> and tries to catch up.